# LETHAL
## Lateral Thinking
## PUZZLES

Paul Sloane & Des MacHale

PUZZLE
WRIGHT
PRESS

An imprint of Sterling
Publishing Co., Inc.
www.puzzlewright.com

Puzzlewright Press and the distinctive Puzzlewright Press logo are
registered trademarks of Sterling Publishing Co., Inc.

The puzzles in this book originally appeared in:
*Captivating Lateral Thinking Puzzles* © 2007 by Paul Sloane and Des MacHale
*Challenging Lateral Thinking Puzzles* © 1992 by Paul Sloane and Des MacHale
*Colorful Lateral Thinking Puzzles* © 2003 by Paul Sloane and Des MacHale
*Cunning Lateral Thinking Puzzles* © 2006 by Paul Sloane and Des MacHale
*Great Lateral Thinking Puzzles* © 1994 by Paul Sloane and Des MacHale
*Improve Your Lateral Thinking* © 1995 by Paul Sloane and Des MacHale
*Ingenious Lateral Thinking Puzzles* © 1998 by Paul Sloane and Des MacHale
*Intriguing Lateral Thinking Puzzles* © 1996 by Paul Sloane and Des MacHale
*Lateral Thinking Puzzlers* © 1991 by Paul Sloane
*Outside-the-Box Lateral Thinking Puzzles* © 2009 by Paul Sloane and Des MacHale
*Outstanding Lateral Thinking Puzzles* © 2005 by Paul Sloane and Des MacHale
*Perplexing Lateral Thinking Puzzles* © 1996 by Paul Sloane and Des MacHale
*Sit & Solve Lateral Thinking Puzzles* © 2003 by Paul Sloane and Des MacHale
*Super Lateral Thinking Puzzles* © 2000 by Paul Sloane and Des MacHale
*Test Your Lateral Thinking IQ* © 1994 by Paul Sloane
*Tricky Lateral Thinking Puzzles* © 1999 by Paul Sloane and Des MacHale

All images used under license from Shutterstock.com

**Library of Congress Cataloging-in-Publication Data**

Sloane, Paul, 1950–
  Lethal lateral thinking puzzles / Paul Sloane & Des MacHale.
     p.  cm.
  Includes bibliographical references and index.
  ISBN 978-1-4027-7881-0 (trade pbk. : alk. paper)
  1. Lateral thinking puzzles.  I. MacHale, Des.  II. Title.
  GV1507.L37S5612   2011
  793.73--dc22

                              2010038934


              2   4   6   8   10   9   7   5   3   1


Published by Sterling Publishing Co., Inc.
387 Park Avenue South, New York, NY 10016
© 2011 by Sterling Publishing Co., Inc.
Distributed in Canada by Sterling Publishing
℅ Canadian Manda Group, 165 Dufferin Street,
Toronto, Ontario, Canada M6K 3H6

*Manufactured in the United States of America*
*All rights reserved*

Sterling ISBN 978-1-4027-7881-0

For information about custom editions, special sales, premium and
corporate purchases, please contact Sterling Special Sales
Department at 800-805-5489 or specialsales@sterlingpublishing.com.

# Acknowledgments

We would like to acknowledge the input and inspiration of many people, including those too numerous to mention by name from all over the world, who have written to us with ideas and encouragement. Also to the contributors to the Lateral Puzzles Forum (www.lateralpuzzles.com) who have given comments and feedback on some early ideas for this book.

This book could not have been produced without the help in editing and reviewing provided by Ann, Jackie, Hannah, and Val Sloane. Also, special thanks to the Broughton family of Brecksville, Ohio for "The Sign," Lizzy Rengel for "His Own Fault," John Faben for "Foolproof," Brian Hobbs for "Death by Reading," Lloyd King for "Getting Away With Murder," and Erwin Brecher for "The Stranger in the Car."

# Contents

· · · · · · · · · · · · · · · · · · · · · · · · · · · · · · · · · · · · · · ·

# Introduction

If you have seen this kind of puzzle before, you will know that it consists of strange situations that require an explanation. They are designed as a form of game for a small group, where one person knows the answer and the others try to figure it out by asking questions. The questions can be answered only by yes, no, or irrelevant. The puzzles can also be used as a form of training because they test and encourage skills in questioning, imagination, inductive reasoning, and lateral thinking.

Sure, some of the situations are implausible. And sure, it is possible to come up with alternative solutions that fit the original puzzle. In fact, you can play a variation of the game where people try to think of as many alternative explanations as possible. But in general, you will get the most enjoyment from these puzzles if you keep questioning until you come up with the answer given in the book. There is a clues section to help out when you get stuck, but the best resource is always your own imagination.

In this book, we have gathered together for you our favorite "lethal" lateral thinking puzzles; i.e., those involving death, murder, accidental killings, and gruesome endings. For some reason or other, they seem to be the most popular puzzles, and like the wonderful novels of Agatha Christie, give rise to the most ingenious solutions.

—Paul Sloane & Des MacHale

# The Puzzles

# Dead Drunk

A man was coming home after a night out drinking. There was no one around, so he decided to relieve himself. Within minutes he was dead. What happened?

*Clues on p. 45/Answer on p. 80*

# Radio Death

A man is driving his car. He turns on the radio and hears music. He stops and shoots himself. Why?

*Clues on p. 45/Answer on p. 80*

# The Archduke

When Archduke Ferdinand was shot in 1914, his attendants were not able to undo his coat to stem his bleeding wound. Why not?

*Clues on p. 45/Answer on p. 80*

# The Big Room

A man is lying dead in a big room. There are musical instruments lying all around. He is holding a bottle of brandy. He died because of the brandy, but how?

*Clues on p. 46*
*Answer on p. 81*

# The Cloth

One man waved a cloth, and another man died. Why?

*Clues on p. 46/Answer on p. 81*

# The Man Who Returned Too Soon

One bright sunny morning a man left his home. After some time he decided to return home and came back directly. When he got home, he died. If he had not gone home so quickly, he would have lived. What happened?

*Clues on p. 46/Answer on p. 81*

# The Perfect Murder

Edward carefully plotted the murder of his wife. One winter's day he strangled her in the bedroom, then faked a burglary. He ransacked the house, scattered possessions, and broke through the patio doors. He set the burglar alarm downstairs before driving to the local golf course to establish his alibi. Two hours later, when Edward was in the middle of his golf game with three colleagues, the burglar alarm went off and the police were alerted. They found the house apparently broken into and the wife strangled. No animals or electrical devices were found which could have set the alarm off, so it looked as though an intruder had set off the alarm before killing the poor woman. Edward was never arrested or charged. The police inspector long suspected Edward, but there was one question which he could not fathom: How did the suspect get the burglar alarm to go off so conveniently? Can you work it out?

*Clues on p. 46/Answer on p. 82*

## One Beautiful Morning

A man woke up on a beautiful summer morning. He went to the window, looked out in horror, and then shot himself. Why?

*Clues on p. 47/Answer on p. 82*

## The Sign

A man and his wife were in their car. The man saw a sign. Without either of them saying a word, he drew a gun and shot his wife dead. Why?

*Clues on p. 47/Answer on p. 83*

## The Truck Driver

A truck driver was driving along an empty highway, when he sensed there was something wrong with his truck. He stopped and got out to look at it. He was then killed. How?

*Clues on p. 47/Answer on p. 83*

# An American Shooting

One American man shot another American man dead in full view of many people. The two men had never met before and did not know each other. Neither was a policeman nor a criminal. The man who shot and killed the other man was not arrested or charged with any crime. Why not?

*Clues on p. 48/Answer on p. 83*

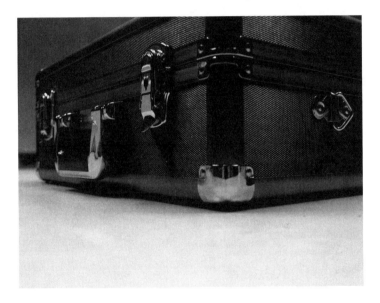

# The Deadly Suitcase

A woman opened a suitcase and found to her horror that there was a body inside. How had it gotten there?

*Clues on p. 48/Answer on p. 84*

# The Flicker

A man was running along a corridor clutching a piece of paper. He saw the lights flicker. He gave a cry of anguish and walked on dejectedly. Why?

*Clues on p. 48/Answer on p. 84*

# The Late Report

A man and his wife went on vacation. Two months later, the man called the police to report the location of a body near the place where he had been on holiday. The police thanked the man and then asked why it had taken him two months to report the body. What was the reason?

*Clues on p. 49/Answer on p. 84*

# The Murderer

Brown told Smith that he had just committed a murder. The two men had never met before. Smith was a responsible citizen and he believed Brown but he did not report him to the police. Why not?

*Clues on p. 49/Answer on p. 85*

# The Plate of Mushrooms

A man enjoyed the taste of mushrooms but had a morbid fear of being poisoned by them, so he never ate them. Yet one day he ordered a large plate of assorted mushrooms to eat. Why?

*Clues on p. 49/Answer on p. 85*

# Death in a Car

A man went out for a drive. A day later he was found dead in the car. The car had not crashed. How had he died?

*Clues on p. 50/Answer on p. 85*

# The Yacht Incident

A yacht is found floating in the middle of the ocean, and around it in the water are a dozen human corpses. Why?

*Clues on p. 50/Answer on p. 86*

# Last Cord

A man lies dead in a field. Next to him is a long piece of cord. How did he die?

*Clues on p. 50/Answer on p. 86*

# The Deadly Shot

A man lay dead in a field. Next to him was a gun. One shot had been fired and because of that shot the man had died. Yet he had not been shot. In fact, there was no wound or mark on his body. How had he died?

*Clues on p. 51/Answer on p. 86*

# The Missing Furniture

A man was doing his job but was killed because he lacked a certain piece of furniture. Why?

*Clues on p. 51/Answer on p. 86*

# The Last Message

A man was found shot dead in his study. He was slumped over his desk and a gun was in his hand. There was a cassette recorder on his desk. When the police entered the room and pressed the play button on the tape recorder they heard, "I can't go on. I have nothing to live for." Then there was the sound of a gunshot. How did the detective immediately know that the man had been murdered?

*Clues on p. 52/Answer on p. 87*

# Death on the Train

A man stepped out of a speeding train to his death. He had been on his own in the compartment, and all that was found there was a very large handkerchief. If he had made the journey by any means other than train, he would almost certainly not have decided to commit suicide. Why did he take his life?

*Clues on p. 52/Answer on p. 87*

# What a Shock

A man woke up. He lit a match. He saw something and died of shock. What was going on?

*Clues on p. 53/Answer on p. 88*

# The Deadly Party

A man went to a party and drank some punch. He then left early. Everyone else at the party who drank the punch subsequently died of poisoning. Why did the man not die?

*Clues on p. 53/Answer on p. 88*

# The Deadly Dresser

A healthy man got dressed and then lay down and died. Why?

*Clues on p. 54/Answer on p. 88*

# The Realization

A man was walking downstairs in a building when he suddenly realized that his wife had just died. How?

*Clues on p. 54/Answer on p. 89*

# The Stranger in the Car

A man and his wife were driving quickly from the suburbs into town when their car ran out of fuel. The man left his wife in the car after telling her to keep the windows closed and the doors locked. When he returned, although the doors and windows were still locked and had remained so throughout, he found his wife dead and a stranger in the car. The car had not been broken into or damaged in any way, and it had no sunroof or hatchback; the only means of entry were the doors. How had the wife died?

*Clues on p. 55/Answer on p. 89*

# False Note

A woman dies and seems to have left a suicide note. How did the police discover that she was in fact murdered?

*Clues on p. 55/Answer on p. 89*

# Swimmer in the Forest

Deep in the forest, a forest ranger found the body of a man dressed only in swimming trunks, snorkel, and facemask. The nearest lake was 8 miles away and the sea was 100 miles away. How did he die?

*Clues on p. 55/Answer on p. 89*

# Anthony and Cleopatra

Anthony and Cleopatra are lying dead on the floor in an Egyptian villa. Nearby is a broken bowl. There are no marks on their bodies and they were not poisoned. They were not alone in the villa when they died. How did they die?

*Clues on p. 56/Answer on p. 90*

# The Rock

A man, going about his business, brushed against a rock. Within minutes he was dead. Why?

*Clues on p. 56/Answer on p. 90*

# The Single Statement

An explorer was captured by a tribe whose chief decided that the man should die. The chief was a very logical man and gave the explorer a choice. The explorer was to make a single statement. If it was true, he would be thrown over a high cliff. If it was false, he would be eaten by lions. What statement did the clever explorer make that forced the chief to let him go?

*Clues on p. 56/Answer on p. 90*

# Death in a Field
. . . . . . . . . . . . . . . . . . . . . . . . . . . . . . . . . . . . . . . .

A man is lying dead in a field. Next to him is an unopened package. There is no other creature in the field. How did he die?

*Clues on p. 57/Answer on p. 91*

# Death in Rome
. . . . . . . . . . . . . . . . . . . . . . . . . . . . . . . . . . . . . . . .

Mr. Jones is reading his daily newspaper. He reads an article with the following headline: "Woman dies in holiday accident." It goes on to say, "Mrs. Rigby-Brown, while on holiday with her husband in Rome, fell to her death from the balcony of her seventh-floor room."

Mr. Jones turns to his wife and says "That was not an accident. It was murder." He had never met either of the Rigby-Browns, so how could he know it was murder?

*Clues on p. 57/Answer on p. 91*

# Dead Man, Dead Dog
. . . . . . . . . . . . . . . . . . . . . .

A man and his dog were found dead in the middle of a field. The man was wearing wading boots. No one else was around. How had they died?

*Clues on p. 58*
*Answer on p. 91*

# The Lonely Man

A man lived alone in a house for two months. Nobody came to visit him and he never went out. At the end of that time, he became deranged. One night he put out the fire, turned off the lights, and walked out of the house. He was never seen or heard of again. His actions in leaving that house resulted in the deaths of 90 people. Why was that?

*Clues on p. 58/Answer on p. 92*

# Asphyxiation

A woman was found gassed in her bedroom. The gas fireplace had been left on. The windows and door were locked from the inside. She had been seen entering the room by her sister. It looked to the police as though she had accidentally put the gas on and forgotten to light it, so they put it down as an accident. In fact, her husband had murdered her. How?

*Clues on p. 59/Answer on p. 92*

# Lethal Action

Brazilian authorities took actions to protect their fruit crops, and ten people from another continent died. How?

*Clues on p. 59/Answer on pp. 92*

# The Man in the Bar

Two brothers were having a drink in a bar. Suddenly, one of the brothers got into a heated argument with the barman. He pulled a knife and, despite his brother's attempts to stop him, stabbed the barman in the chest.

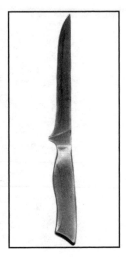

At his trial, he was found guilty of assault with a deadly weapon and grievous bodily harm. At the end of the trial, the judge said "You have been found guilty of a vicious crime. However, I have no choice but to set you free." Why?

*Clues on p. 60*
*Answer on p. 93*

# The Man in the Bar, Again!

A man walked into a bar and asked for a drink. The barman had never met the man before but without saying a word he pulled out a gun and shot him dead. Why?

*Clues on p. 60/Answer on p. 93*

# Poisoned

An old man was poisoned. The police found that he had eaten and drunk nothing on the day of his death. How had the poison been administered?

*Clues on p. 61/Answer on p. 94*

# Slow Death

The ancient Greek playwright Aeschylus was killed by a tortoise. How?

*Clues on p. 61/Answer on p. 94*

# Murder

An elderly woman is found dead in her bed. She has been murdered. In her bedroom is a fine collection of plates. The police established that she was in good health, seemed perfectly fine when she went shopping the day before, and that no one else had recently visited or entered the house. How did she die?

*Clues on p. 61/Answer on p. 94*

# A Shooting

........................................................

At a party two men, Rob and Bill, became engaged in a violent quarrel. Rob pulled a gun and, in plain view of many witnesses, shot Bill dead. The police were called. They questioned Rob and the witnesses. They decided that it was a case of murder, yet they pressed no charge against Rob. Why not?

*Clues on p. 62/Answer on p. 95*

# The Nonchalant Wife

........................................................

A woman came home one evening and switched on the light in her living room. She was horrified to see the remains of her husband lying on the floor. He had committed suicide. Ignoring the situation, the woman had a cup of coffee and went calmly about her housework, and did not phone for medical assistance or the police. Why not?

*Clues on p. 62/Answer on p. 95*

# Death of a Player

A sportsman was rushed to a hospital from where he was playing and died shortly afterward. Why?

*Clues on p. 62/Answer on p. 95*

# Stealth Weapon?

A woman murders her spouse and doesn't leave the house. The police arrive the next day but can't find the murder weapon. Why not?

*Clues on p. 63/Answer on p. 95*

# Bingo

A man hears a woman calling out what he thinks is a number, and he immediately dies. What was the number?

*Clues on p. 63/Answer on p. 96*

# Strangulation

A famous dancer was found strangled. The police did not suspect murder. Why not?

*Clues on p. 63/Answer on p. 96*

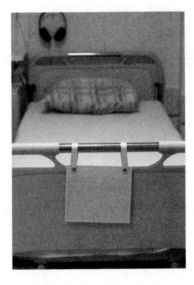

# The Unlucky Bed

A certain bed in a certain hospital acquires the reputation of being unlucky. Whatever patient is assigned to this bed seems to die there on a Friday evening. A watch is kept by camera and the reason is discovered. What is it?

*Clues on p. 64*
*Answer on p. 96*

# Blood

A man lies dead in a room. There is no visible mark on his body, but there are spots of blood on the walls. How did he die?

*Clues on p. 64/Answer on p. 97*

# Shooting a Dead Man

A policeman shot a dead man. He was not acting illegally. Why did he do it?

*Clues on p. 64/Answer on p. 97*

# The Deadly Melody

A woman heard a tune that she recognized. She took a gun and shot a stranger. Why?

*Clues on p. 65/Answer on p. 98*

# The Cabin

In the mountains there is a cabin. Inside, three people lie dead. The cabin is locked from the inside and there is no sign of struggle or of any weapons. What happened?

*Clues on p. 65/Answer on p. 98*

# Biography

An author died because he wrote a biography. How did he die?

*Clues on p. 66/Answer on p. 99*

# The Fish

A man saw a fish, and because of that he shot himself. Why?

*Clues on p. 66/Answer on p. 99*

# The Broken Bag

A healthy woman died because the plastic bag she was carrying broke. There were many people around her at the time but they were completely unharmed. What happened?

*Clues on p. 66/Answer on p. 100*

# By the Pool

A man was lying dead next to a swimming pool. There was a towel around his face. How had he died?

*Clues on p. 67/Answer on p. 100*

# Putt Out

A golfer died because he holed a putt. How come?

*Clues on p. 67/Answer on p. 100*

# Stranded

A man is found dead on a little island—he is the only person on the island. He did not die of starvation, he did not commit suicide, he was not killed by a wild animal, and he did not die of poisoning or thirst. There are no trees on the tiny bare island. How did he die?

*Clues on p. 67/Answer on p. 101*

# Foolproof

Bob wrote a story. He died. Sharon read the story. Her husband died. The story was never read again. Why not?

*Clues on p. 67*
*Answer on p. 101*

# The Tracks of My Tires

The police found a murder victim and they noticed a pair of tire tracks leading to and from the body. They followed the tracks to a nearby farmhouse where two men and a woman were sitting on the porch. There was no car at the farmhouse and none of the three could drive. The police arrested the woman. Why?

*Clues on p. 68/Answer on p. 101*

# The Deadly Stone

A man shot himself because he saw a stone with a small drop of blood on it. Why?

*Clues on p. 68/Answer on p. 102*

# The Upset Woman

When the woman saw him she was upset. Even though she had never seen him before, she had left some food for him because she knew he would be hungry. But he could not reach the food because he had an iron bar across his back. He died soon after and the woman was pleased. What's going on?

*Clues on p. 68/Answer on p. 102*

# His Own Fault

If he hadn't stolen the wallet, he would have lived longer.

*Clues on p. 68/Answer on p. 102*

# Stamp Dearth Death

A man died because he didn't buy enough stamps. What happened?

*Clues on p. 69/Answer on p. 103*

# Murder Mystery

A woman murders her husband. She gains no advantage for herself in doing so. The police knew she did it. She was never charged with murder. What was going on?

*Clues on p. 69/Answer on p. 103*

# The Deadly Deal

A woman looks in through a window and sees two men sitting at a table. Both of them are dead. One man has a gun in his hand and the other man has a pack of playing cards in his hand. What had happened?

*Clues on p. 69/Answer on p. 103*

# Getting Away With Murder

A security guard in a hotel sees a man go into a room in which there is no one else present and which may only be accessed through a single doorway. Several minutes later he sees a woman enter the room and immediately scream. Lying dead in a pool of blood in the room is the man, murdered. But how did the killer get into and out of the room without being seen by the guard, who had remained on the same spot and watchful throughout?

*Clues on p. 70/Answer on p. 104*

# Pack Man

A man is found dead in a forest with a pack on his back. What happened?

*Clues on p. 70/Answer on p. 104*

# Murderous Intent

A woman meets the man of her dreams at her mother's funeral but she neglects to get his name, address, or any other contact details. A few days later she kills her sister. Why?

*Clues on p. 70/Answer on p. 104*

# More Murderous Intent

A man wanted to commit suicide by shooting himself. His life insurance policy paid out if he died by accident or was murdered but not if he committed suicide. How did he make his death look like murder rather than suicide?

*Clues on p. 71/Answer on p. 104*

# The Deadly Sculpture

A penniless sculptor made a beautiful metal statue, which he sold. Because of this he died soon afterward. Why?

*Clues on p. 71/Answer on p. 105*

# Shot Dead

A woman who was in a house saw a stranger walking down the road. She took a gun and shot him dead. The next day she did the same thing to another stranger. Other people saw her do it and knew that she had killed the two men, yet she was never arrested or charged. Why?

*Clues on p. 72/Answer on p. 105*

## The Fatal Fish

A man was preparing a fish to eat for a meal when he made a mistake. He then knew that he would shortly die. How?

*Clues on p. 72/Answer on p. 105*

# The Deadly Drawing

A woman walked into a room and saw a new picture there. She immediately knew that someone had been killed. How?

*Clues on p. 72/Answer on p. 106*

# Give Us a Hand ...

A man searching for precious stones didn't find any, but found a severed human hand instead. What had happened?

*Clues on p. 73/Answer on p. 106*

# The Fatal Fall

A woman dropped a piece of wood. She picked it up again and carried on as if nothing had happened. The wood was not damaged and she was not injured, but the incident cost her her life. Why?

*Clues on p. 73/Answer on p. 106*

# Death by Reading

She died because she was a voracious reader. How come?

*Clues on p. 73/Answer on p. 107*

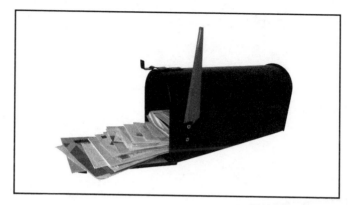

## Deadly Delivery

A man was killed, and as a result, the post office has had to deliver millions more pieces of mail. Who was he?

*Clues on p. 74/Answer on p. 107*

## Lifesaver

A man held a newspaper very close to his chest in order to save his life. How?

*Clues on p. 74/Answer on p. 108*

## The Lethal Lie

A man was captured and interrogated. His captors tell him, truthfully, that if he answers their questions truthfully, his life will be spared. Although he answers their questions truthfully, they immediately shoot him dead. Why?

*Clues on p. 74/Answer on pp. 108-109*

# Broken Match

A man is found dead in a field. He is clutching a broken match. What happened?

*Clues on p. 75/Answer on p. 109*

# The Man Who Hanged Himself

Not far from Madrid, there is a large wooden barn. The barn is completely empty except for a dead man hanging from the central rafter. The rope around his neck is ten feet long and his feet are three feet off the ground. The nearest wall is 20 feet away. It is not possible to climb up the walls or along the rafters, yet he still managed to hang himself. How did he do it?

*Clues on p. 75/Answer on p. 110*

# The Music Stopped

The music stopped. She died. Explain.

*Clues on p. 75/Answer on p. 110*

# Suicide

A man wakes up in a dark room. He switches on the light. A few minutes later he shoots himself. Why?

*Clues on p. 76/Answer on p. 111*

# The False Confession

A man confessed to a murder he did not commit. He received the death penalty and it was carried out. Why did he confess?

*Clues on p. 77/Answer on p. 111*

# The Clues

## Dead Drunk

- He died an accidental death as a result of his actions and where he was.

- He was alone at a subway station.

## Radio Death

- He had been expecting to hear the piece of music that he heard, but had not planned to commit suicide.

- There was something about the way the music was playing that meant that he was in very serious trouble.

## The Archduke

- He was very vain.

- His coat had no buttons or zippers.

## The Big Room

- He died because he went back for the brandy.

- He drowned.

## The Cloth

- The man who waved the cloth knew that his action would probably cause a man to die.

- He did not know which man would die.

- The man died of a gunshot.

## The Man Who Returned Too Soon

- He died an accidental death. No other person or creature was involved.

- The danger was not in his home. The fact that he returned too quickly killed him.

## The Perfect Murder

- He had caused something to fall so that its motion would be detected by the burglar alarm sensors.

- No electrical, telephone, or radio devices were used. He did not use any spring or complex mechanical device. He used something much simpler.

## One Beautiful Morning

- The man did not see anything unusual, terrible, or frightening from the window.

- He committed suicide because it was a beautiful morning.

- He had done something terrible which he now regretted.

- He was a religious leader.

## The Sign

- The sign was inside the car and the car was stationary.

- He shot her because he learned she had been having an affair.

## The Truck Driver

- He was killed accidentally. No other person or creature was involved.

- He had sensed that something was wrong with his truck. He was right. His death and the problem with the truck were linked.

## An American Shooting

- Although an innocent man was killed, no crime was committed.

- Both men were armed.

- This took place in the 19th century.

## The Deadly Suitcase

- The body was that of a child who had died accidentally through suffocation.

- The woman was poor and had tried to save money.

## The Flicker

- He knew that someone had died.

- The piece of paper could have saved a life.

# The Late Report

- The man was not involved in any way in the death of the person whose body he had reported.

- The man had not noticed the body earlier, but did later.

# The Murderer

- Brown had in fact committed the murder. He was not lying.

- Brown told Smith about the murder in all seriousness and with full detail.

- Smith was the first person to hear this or know that Brown had committed the murder.

- Smith had nothing to gain from the murder. He was not a criminal, simply an honest and socially responsible citizen.

# The Plate of Mushrooms

- He still believed that one or more of the mushrooms might be poisonous.

- However, he was no longer concerned that the mushrooms might kill him.

# Death in a Car

- His death was an accident, not murder or suicide.

- Neither he nor the car was unusual in any way.

- He knew he was going to die, but only just before he died.

- The car was stationary immediately before, during, and after his death.

- There were no wounds or marks on his body, and no other person or animal was involved.

- The location where he parked the car was critical.

# The Yacht Incident

- They had been passengers aboard the yacht.

- They died because of an accident. They drowned.

# Last Cord

- He was not strangled by the cord.

- His death was an accident.

- No other human or animal caused his death

- His death was violent.

- The cord was a special kind of cord, and it was broken.

## The Deadly Shot

- It does not matter what the man was shooting at, and it is irrelevant whether or not he hit his intended target.

- No other human or animal was involved in his death.

- He knew he was going to die before he died, but not before he fired the gun.

## The Missing Furniture

- He did not fall to his death, but his death was accidental.

- The piece of furniture was very common—it was not heavy or unusual in any way.

- His job was unusual and dangerous.

# The Last Message

- The man had been murdered, and the scene had been made to look like a suicide.

- There was nothing about the room, the desk, or the gun that indicated to the detective that it was murder.

- The clue was in the cassette recording.

- It had nothing to do with the man's voice or accent.

# Death on the Train

- The man did not feel suicidal when he boarded the train. Something happened on the train that caused him to take his life.

- No one else was involved.

- The man was recently discharged from the hospital.

- He committed suicide because he mistakenly thought that he had not been cured.

## What a Shock

- The man saw another person.

- The person he saw was not alive.

- He expected to see someone else. He now knew that he would soon die.

## The Deadly Party

- The man did not poison the other people.

- Nothing was added to the punch after he left.

- There was nothing wrong with the glasses, the ladle, or the punch bowl itself.

- There was nothing special about the man who left early that made him immune to the poison. If anyone else had left early, they also would have survived.

## The Deadly Dresser

- If he had not dressed, he would not have died.

- He died by accident.

- He was poisoned.

## The Realization

- The man's wife had died, and it was an accidental death.

- She was in the same building as he was, but she was on another floor—well outside his sight and hearing range.

- He saw something that caused him to realize she had died

- Nothing major like a fire or explosion killed her. Other people near her did not die.

# The Stranger in the Car

- There was nothing odd or special about the car. It was a regular four-door family car.

- The stranger was a male human being.

- The woman's death was neither murder nor suicide; it was accidental.

- She did not die of poisoning, suffocation, or heart attack.

- The stranger was the cause of the woman's death, although not deliberately.

# False Note

- She apparently wrote a note to a friend saying she was going to end it all.

- The police examined the note carefully.

- It was impossible to tell if it was her hand that had written the note.

# Swimmer in the Forest

- The man died at the spot where he was found.

- He had previously been swimming.

- He was taken to the forest against his will.

- However, he was not deliberately taken there; it was an accident.

# Anthony and Cleopatra

- This is an old one. It can prove a little difficult if you have not heard it before.

- The most fruitful lines of questioning are those that try to establish the exact cause and circumstances of death. To cut a long story short, it can be said that their deaths followed the accidental breaking of the bowl. The bowl had contained water. They died from lack of oxygen.

# The Rock

- He was uninjured, but the rock damaged his suit.

# The Single Statement

- The explorer must make a statement that is both true and false at the same time. Better still, it should be a statement that means that any action the chief takes would place him in the position of having acted illogically.

- Can you construct a statement about the way the explorer will die that is neither true nor false?

## Death in a Field

- His death was an accident.

- He died in the field, right where he lies.

- No one else was present in or around the field at the time.

- If he had been able to open the package, that would have saved him.

- He knew he was going to die as he entered the field.

## Death in Rome

- Mr. Jones was right in saying that it was murder.

- Mr. Rigby-Brown was the murderer.

- Mr. Jones had never communicated in any way with Mrs. Rigby-Brown.

- Mr. Jones, in his professional capacity, had provided a service to Mr. Rigby-Brown.

- Mr. Jones deduced from this service and the newspaper article that Mrs. Rigby-Brown had been murdered.

# Dead Man, Dead Dog

- The man had been fishing illegally in a lake.

- In desperation the man had run away from the lake, but to no avail.

- The dog was a retriever.

# The Lonely Man

- What he did after leaving the house is not relevant.

- He could have left the house earlier.

- It was not an ordinary sort of house.

- He performed a function within the house, and the cessation of this function was the cause of the deaths of the 90 people.

- The 90 people were involved in some form of travel when they died.

## Asphyxiation

- No one other than the woman entered the room.
- She died from breathing gas.
- She had lit the fireplace.
- The fireplace was not faulty in any way.

## Lethal Action

- The dead people were from Africa. They didn't eat the fruit.
- The Brazilian authorities' actions involved pesticides.
- The deaths of the people from Africa were accidents.
- They had acted illegally.

# The Man in the Bar

- The man was really guilty of the crimes.
- The brothers were not identical twins.
- It was not a case of mistaken identity.
- The man was not physically normal.
- The judge chose to not send the man to prison because of his brother.

# The Man in the Bar, Again!

- The barman neither knew nor recognized the man.
- However, the barman thought he recognized the man.
- The barman deliberately shot the man.
- The barman's motive was revenge.
- The barman was initially pleased that he had shot the man, but he later regretted it.

## Poisoned

- He had followed his normal daily routine unaware that someone had planned to poison him. He had met no one else on the day of his murder.

- He had inadvertently put the poison in his mouth.

## Slow Death

- Aeschylus did not trip over or slip on the tortoise.

- He did not eat it or attempt to eat it. He was not poisoned or bitten by the tortoise.

- No other human was involved in his death.

## Murder

- The police discovered that she had been poisoned. They tested all the food and drink in the house and found no trace of poison.

- She had bought many fine plates, but rarely went to shops or markets.

- The day before her death she had been to the grocery store and the post office.

# A Shooting

- Rob was not a police officer, nor was he acting in self-defense.

- Bill was not a criminal. His murder was in no way justified.

- Rob had had no intention of killing Bill. The police were satisfied that someone other than Rob was the murderer.

- Their professions are important.

# The Nonchalant Wife

- Even though she found her husband's remains on the floor, the woman had no reason to call any authorities.

- The woman was horrified to see her husband's remains on the floor, but not at all surprised that he was dead.

# Death of a Player

- The man was not involved in any collisions or tackles and did not suffer any injuries, yet it was because of his sport that he accidentally died.

- He was a golfer, but he was not hit by a club or a ball or indeed by anything.

- If only he had put his tee in his pocket!

## Stealth Weapon?

- She did not throw the weapon away or hide it anywhere.

- She was not able to get rid of the weapon immediately, but a day was enough time for her to dispose of it.

## Bingo

- The woman was trying to warn the man.

- The number the man thought he heard is pretty small. Start counting!

## Strangulation

- She was strangled to death with a scarf.

- No dancing was involved.

- She should not have been in such a hurry.

## The Unlucky Bed

- All the patients who died were seriously ill, but they were not expected to die.

- There is nothing wrong or dangerous about the bed or its location.

- No doctors or nurses are involved in the cause of the deaths.

- Everyone who died had been receiving the same specific sort of treatment.

## Blood

- The blood was his blood.

- No other people were present at the time of his death.

- He was not murdered, but those responsible for his death left the blood marks.

## Shooting a Dead Man

- The policeman knew that the man was already dead.

- He wanted someone else to see what he was doing.

- He was not tampering with evidence.

- He was trying to get information.

## The Deadly Melody

- She was in her home when this happened.

- She had heard the tune many times before. Normally she was happy when she heard this tune.

- The stranger was trying to rob her.

## The Cabin

- All three died at the same time. Their deaths were violent but accidental.

- They knew they were going to die immediately before they died. They died because they were in the cabin. If they had gotten out of the cabin three hours earlier they would have lived. If they had gotten out three minutes earlier they would still have died.

# Biography

- His death was accidental.

- Had he chosen a different subject for a biography, he would not have died.

- The author died a similar death to that suffered by the subject of his biography.

## The Fish

- The fish was sent to him.

- The fish was a signal.

- He knew that he was bound to die.

## The Broken Bag

- The woman was traveling on a plane when this happened.

- The plastic bag contained drugs.

# By the Pool

- He had died accidentally. No one else was involved in his death. His death had nothing to do with swimming or drowning.

- He had put the towel around his face before his death in an effort to help him survive.

- Had he reached the pool, he would have lived.

# Putt Out

- The golfer was thrilled to sink the putt.

- There were other people watching and he acknowledged their applause.

- He was killed in a tragic accident.

- If he had missed the putt, he would have lived, but someone else might have died.

# Stranded

- He was the only person on the island.

- He expected to be safe there.

- He was killed violently.

# Foolproof

- Bob was a brilliant writer.

- Bob was murdered.

- Sharon's husband was murdered.

# The Tracks of My Tires

- The police didn't ask any questions but merely used their powers of observation.

- When the police arrived, none of the three suspects was carrying a weapon or wearing blood-stained clothing.

- The police correctly deduced that the woman was the murderer.

# The Deadly Stone

- The blood on the stone was the man's blood. It had been put there two days before his death.

- Nobody else was involved.

- He had marked the stone with his blood for a purpose.

# The Upset Woman

- He was an unwelcome intruder.

- He had visited before, so she left some food for him.

- She wanted him to die.

# His Own Fault

- The man was a criminal.

- He died because he stole a wallet.

- He died following a car accident.

# Stamp Dearth Death

- If he had bought the right postage, he would have lived.

- He sent a package.

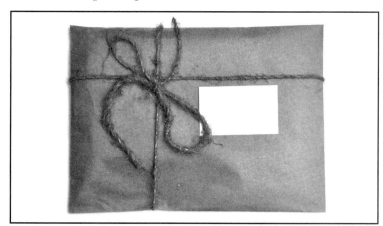

# Murder Mystery

- Both the husband and wife had been married before.

- Their marriage was successful and neither was unfaithful to the other.

- She killed her husband to help someone she loved.

# The Deadly Deal

- They had been playing cards, but not as a game.

- One man had shot himself.

- They knew they were going to die.

# Getting Away With Murder

- The man did not kill himself. He was stabbed to death.

- The murderer was neither the woman nor the guard.

- The murderer entered and left the room.

- There was just one door and there were no windows or other entrances to the room.

- The room was very small.

# Pack Man

- This has nothing to do with planes or parachutes (that's a different puzzle!)

- His death was accidental and violent.

- The pack killed him directly but he was not poisoned, drowned, or crushed.

# Murderous Intent

- She did not do this for any kind of financial gain.

- She had a seemingly rational reason for the cold-blooded murder of her sister.

- She was interested in the man she met at the funeral but she did not see her sister as a rival.

## More Murderous Intent

- The man shot himself in a park. He waited until there was no one around.

- No one assisted him in any way.

- He knew that if the gun were found next to his body it would look like suicide.

## The Deadly Sculpture

- He lived a lonely life in a remote building.

- He made the statue out of copper. It was taken far away and he never saw it again.

- He died as the result of an accident.

- No other person or animal (or sculpture) was involved.

## Shot Dead

- The woman and the strangers were neither criminals nor police.

- The strangers did not see the woman and did not know that she was in the house.

- The strangers were armed and were a threat to the woman.

## The Fatal Fish

- The man died in an accident. He was not poisoned or stabbed.

- No other person was involved. No crime was involved.

- The man did not eat the fish. The type of fish is irrelevant. It was dead.

- He was not indoors.

## The Deadly Drawing

- She was correct in her deduction that someone had been killed.

- She did not know the person who had been killed, nor who had killed the person, nor how the person had died.

- She had never been in that room before and she had not seen the picture before.

# Give Us a Hand ...

- The man whose hand it was had also been looking for precious stones.
- He had been forced to cut off his own hand.
- To find these precious stones, men needed strong limbs, good eyes, good lungs, and great fitness.

# The Fatal Fall

- The woman wasn't a criminal, and no crime was involved.
- She was quite upset to have dropped the piece of wood.
- The wood was a cylinder about one foot long.
- The piece of wood was not particularly valuable and could easily be replaced.
- Many people saw her drop the piece of wood.

# Death by Reading

- She read books and magazines.
- The topic of her reading is not relevant.
- She was murdered by her husband.
- She was poisoned.

# Deadly Delivery

- The man had nothing to do with the mail or post office.

- The extra mail was not informing people about the man or his death.

- He was a good person but not especially important in his day.

## Lifesaver

- The newspaper did not directly protect him from a weapon or from danger.

- It did not stanch a wound.

- It was that same day's newspaper, and it served as information that helped save him.

## The Lethal Lie

- Criminals who wanted to know where some money was hidden interrogated the man.

- He answered truthfully and told where the money was.

- The criminals and the man were deceived.

- There was a language issue.

# Broken Match

- The match was instrumental in the man's death.
- The man was not trying to light something with the match prior to his death.
- The man was alone in the field.
- The man knew he was going to die before he entered the field.
- The man was not murdered.
- The man fell into the field.

# The Man Who Hanged Himself

- There was nobody else involved before, during, or after his suicide.
- He stood on something in order to reach the rafter.
- That something has now gone, but no one took it away.

# The Music Stopped

- She died because the music stopped.
- The music was a signal.
- She was doing something dangerous at the time.
- She worked in the field of entertainment.

# Suicide

- He awoke naturally—he was not awakened by any noise or action.

- He committed suicide because something happened that caused him to realize something.

- The realization was caused by something he heard, not something he saw.

- There was no one else in the house.

- It was a special kind of house.

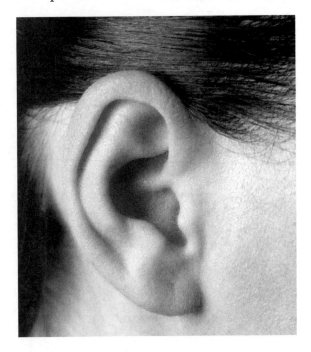

# The False Confession

- He made a perfectly rational decision.

- Several other people benefited from his decision.

- He was protecting the real murderer. He did not like the murderer and they were not related.

- We all have to die someday.

# The Answers

# Dead Drunk

He was at a deserted underground railway station. He urinated onto the electrified third rail and was electrocuted.

# Radio Death

The man is a disc jockey who put on a long piece of music during his show and slipped out of the studio in order to kill his wife. He had timed the plan perfectly and would claim that he was on the air throughout the evening as his alibi. After killing the woman, he drove hurriedly back and turned on the radio. He heard the music repeating as the record skipped. He knew that his cover was blown, and he shot himself.

# The Archduke

Archduke Ferdinand's uniform was sewn onto him so that he looked immaculately smart. It could not be removed quickly. His desire for a perfect appearance probably cost him his life.

## The Big Room

The large room is the ballroom of the *Titanic*. The barman went back to get a bottle of brandy for the lifeboat, but he never made it.

## The Cloth

The man who died was shot in a duel. The man who waved the cloth gave the signal that the two duelists could commence.

## The Man Who Returned Too Soon

His home was a houseboat on the sea. He put on his scuba gear and dived 200 feet. One should ascend from such a depth slowly in order to depressurize. He came up too quickly and suffered a severe attack of the bends, from which he died.

# The Perfect Murder

Edward placed a tray on the edge of the kitchen table. He put some pans on one side of the tray and ice cubes on the other side. When the ice eventually melted, the weight of the pans caused the tray to fall off the table. The pans bounced on the floor and the alarm was activated. To the police, the tray, pans, and water looked to be part of the general disturbance in the kitchen.

# One Beautiful Morning

The man was the leader of a religious cult. Believing that the world would end that night he had offered his followers the choice of taking poison or seeing the destruction of the world. Many, including his own children, had chosen poison. He and others had gone to sleep expecting to wake to Armageddon. When the next day dawned as a beautiful summer morning he knew that he had made a terrible mistake.

## The Sign

The car was stationary. The man's wife was deaf and mute. She used sign language to tell her husband that she was having an affair with another man and that she was leaving him.

## The Truck Driver

One of the wheels of the truck had worked loose and come off a little earlier. It had continued to roll along the road. As he stood by his truck, he was hit by the runaway wheel.

## An American Shooting

This happened during the American Civil War. The men were soldiers in the opposing armies.

## The Deadly Suitcase

The body was that of the woman's son. They were flying to the U.S. to start a new life, but she did not have enough money for two airfares. She put him in a suitcase with tiny airholes. She did not know that the luggage compartment would be depressurized.

## The Flicker

The man was carrying a stay of execution for a condemned man who was due to die in the electric chair. When he saw the lights flicker, he knew that he was too late.

## The Late Report

The man saw the body in the background on one of his vacation photographs. It was two months before the film was developed.

## The Murderer

Brown confessed to Father Smith in the confessional. Father Smith was prevented from telling the police by the seal of the confessional.

## The Plate of Mushrooms

He was to be executed. The mushrooms were his last meal.

## Death in a Car

The man drove his car to the beach to watch the sunset over the waves. He fell asleep. The tide came in and seeped in around the car doors and windows. He awoke, but with the pressure of the water, he couldn't get out of the car. The water filled the car and drowned him. Later the tide went out and he was found dead in an empty car.

# The Yacht Incident

All of the people on the yacht went swimming. No one put a rope ladder over the side. They were unable to get back on board again.

## Last Cord

Incredible as it may seem, some people enjoy leaping off high buildings or bridges with a length of elastic cord fastened to them. This pastime is known as bungee jumping. The poor man in this situation died when he jumped from a high crane in the field and his bungee cord broke.

## The Deadly Shot

The man died through suffocation. He was covered by an avalanche of snow which had been started by the sound of his gunshot as he stood at the foot of a snow-covered mountain.

## The Missing Furniture

The man was a circus lion tamer who had unfortunately forgotten his chair when he had to face a bad-tempered lion!

# The Last Message

The cassette had started at the beginning of the man's utterance. Who could have rewound it?

## Death on the Train

The man had just completed a course of treatment intended to cure him of blindness. He had high hopes of success. He traveled home on the train with the handkerchief as a blindfold to protect his eyes from the light.

He could not wait and decided to remove the blindfold to test his eyesight. When he removed the blindfold, he could see nothing and assumed that the treatment had failed. He could not face the future as a blind man and, therefore, he stepped out of the speeding train to his death.

The treatment had, in fact, been successful, but he had unfortunately removed the blindfold while the train was in a long tunnel. The carriage was in complete darkness.

## What a Shock

The man was a prisoner who had been condemned to a very long jail sentence. He paid the prison undertaker to help him escape. The plan was that when the next prisoner died, the man would get into the coffin with the corpse. Later, after the coffin was buried outside the prison walls, the undertaker would dig it up to release the man.

When he heard that a man had died, the prisoner put his plan into action. In the dead of night he climbed into the coffin with the corpse. He fell asleep. He awoke after the burial and lit a match. He then saw that the face of the corpse was that of the undertaker!

## The Deadly Party

The poison in the punch came from the ice cubes in it. When the man drank from the punch the ice had just been added and was still solid. Gradually, during the course of the evening, the ice melted contaminating the punch with the poison.

## The Deadly Dresser

The last thing he put on was his shoe, and it contained a deadly spider that bit him. He died soon after.

## The Realization

The man had just visited his wife in a hospital. She was on a life-support machine following a car accident. As he was walking down the stairs all the lights went out. There had been a power cut and the emergency backup systems had failed. He knew immediately that his wife had died.

## The Stranger in the Car

The woman had died in childbirth. The stranger was the man's newborn son.

## False Note

The note was an e-mail sent from the woman's PC. However, the police noticed that it was sent after the time she was known to have died.

## Swimmer in the Forest

During a forest fire some months earlier, a firefighting plane had scooped up water from the lake to drop on the fire. The plane had accidentally picked up the unfortunate swimmer.

## Anthony and Cleopatra

Anthony and Cleopatra were goldfish. They died when their bowl was knocked over by a rather clumsy guard dog.

## The Rock

The man was a deep-sea diver. The sharp rock punctured his suit.

## The Single Statement

The explorer made the statement, "I will be eaten by lions." Now, if the chief does feed him to the lions, his statement will have been true, so he should have been thrown off the cliff. But if he is thrown off the cliff, his statement will have been false. The chief had to admit that the only fair course of action was to let the explorer go free.

## Death in a Field

The man had jumped from a plane, but his parachute had failed to open. It was the unopened package by his side.

## Death in Rome

Mr. Jones was a travel agent. He had recently supplied by mail two plane tickets for a Mr. Rigby-Brown. The two tickets were for Rome, but the one for Mr. Rigby-Brown had been ordered as a round-trip ticket. Mrs. Rigby-Brown's ticket had been one-way only.

## Dead Man, Dead Dog

The field was next to a lake. The man had been poaching fish by dynamiting them. He threw a stick of dynamite into the lake. Unfortunately, the dog chased the stick, retrieved it, and carried it to the man, who had run away across the field—but to no avail.

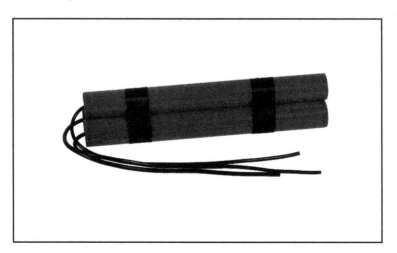

# The Lonely Man

He was a lighthouse keeper, and the house in which he lived was a lighthouse on a remote outcrop of rock. When he left the place and turned the lights off, the warning to incoming ships was removed. A shipwreck occurred that resulted in the deaths of 90 people.

## Asphyxiation

The woman lit the fireplace and then fell asleep on the bed. Her husband simply turned off the main gas supply into the house and then turned it on again a few moments later. This caused the fire to go out. The gas then filled the room and asphyxiated the unfortunate woman.

## Lethal Action

The Brazilian customs authorities require that all imported fruit be sprayed with pesticides to prevent insects or diseases from reaching domestic crops. They sprayed the hold of a fruit ship arriving from the Ivory Coast in Africa just before it docked in Brazil. They subsequently found the bodies of 10 stowaways who had hidden in the ship's hold and who had been poisoned by the pesticides.

# The Man in the Bar

The guilty man was a Siamese twin, joined at the waist to his brother. The judge could not send the guilty twin to prison without unfairly sentencing the innocent brother.

## The Man in the Bar, Again!

The barman's daughter had been murdered by the identical twin of the man who entered the bar. The murderer had been acquitted because of a technicality (e.g., an illegal search by the police). So the barman longed for revenge. He had seen the murderer in court. He did not know that the murderer had a twin, and, consequently, he shot an innocent man who had entered his bar by chance.

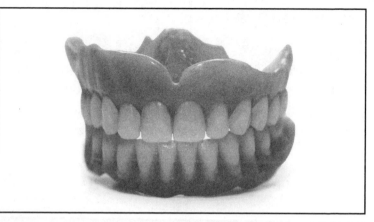

## Poisoned

The poison had been put on his false teeth.

## Slow Death

Aeschylus was killed when the tortoise was dropped on him from a height by an eagle who may have mistaken the bald head of Aeschylus for a rock on which to break the tortoise.

## Murder

The elderly woman was poisoned by her greedy nephew, who wanted to inherit her fortune. He sent her what looked like a mailer with a fantastic offer for a collector plate, which he knew she would want to have. To order the plate, the offer had to be completed, folded and sealed, and sent back without delay. The nephew had put a slow-acting poison on the seal of the mailer. Once his aunt had licked the seal and posted the mailer, there was nothing to connect him to her murder.

## A Shooting

Rob and Bill were actors playing out a scene for a television crime series. Unbeknown to Rob, someone with a grudge against Bill had substituted real bullets for the blanks that should have been in Rob's gun.

## The Nonchalant Wife

The woman's husband had committed suicide three years earlier. The cat had knocked over the urn containing his ashes. After she finished her cup of coffee, she swept his remains back into an urn.

## Death of a Player

The man was a golfer who absentmindedly sucked on his tee between shots. The tee had picked up deadly weed killer used on the golf course, and the man died from poisoning.

## Stealth Weapon?

The woman hit her husband on the head with a solidly frozen chicken. She then cooked and ate the "weapon."

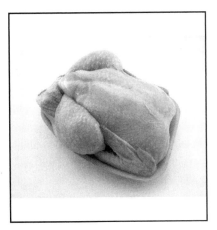

## Bingo

The number the man heard was 4 ("Fore!"). The man was hit on the head by a golf ball and killed.

## Strangulation

The famous dancer was Isadora Duncan, who was strangled when the long scarf she was wearing caught in the wheel of her sports car.

## The Unlucky Bed

Every Friday morning, a cleaning woman comes to the ward with a vacuum cleaner. The most convenient electrical socket is the one to which the patient's life support machine is connected. She unplugs this for a few minutes while she does her work. The noise of the vacuum cleaner covers the patient's dying gasps. The cleaner reconnects the machine and goes to the next ward.

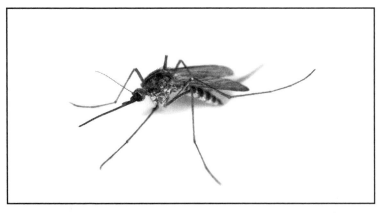

## Blood

The man went to Africa to study local wildlife. He lived in a small hut deep in the wilderness. He frequently got bitten by mosquitoes, which he crushed against the wall. Eventually, he realized that he had caught malaria from the mosquitoes, but he was too isolated to go for help.

## Shooting a Dead Man

This puzzle is based on an incident in *The Untouchables*. There had been a shootout at a house and the police had captured a gangster who was refusing to give them the information they wanted. Sean Connery went outside and propped up against the window the body of another gangster, who had died earlier. Pretending the man was alive, he threatened him and then shot him. The prisoner was convinced that Connery would stop at nothing to get the information he wanted. The prisoner talked.

# The Deadly Melody

The woman was alone and asleep in her house in the middle of the night when she was awakened by the sound of her musical jewel box. She knew that a burglar was in her bedroom. She reached under her pillow, pulled out a gun and shot him.

# The Cabin

It is a plane cabin. The plane crashed, killing both pilots and the passenger.

# Biography

The author wrote the biography of Marie Curie, the great French scientist who made many important discoveries concerning radioactivity. She won two Nobel prizes but died of leukemia caused by radiation. The biographer collected many of her writings, belongings, and experimental apparatuses to help him write about her. Unfortunately, most of the memorabilia were highly contaminated with radioactivity, and he died later as a result of being exposed to it. Radiation was not known to be dangerous to one's health until later.

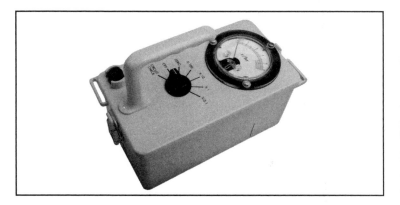

# The Fish

The man was under a death threat because he had been a prosecution witness in a Mafia trial. In order to escape he had been given a different identity and had set up a new life for himself. The sending of a dead fish is a traditional Mafia death threat. When he received the dead fish in the mail, the man knew that the Mafia had uncovered his identity and that he would surely be killed.

# The Broken Bag

The woman was a drug courier or "mule." She had swallowed numerous condoms filled with heroin before boarding a flight for London. One condom split inside her and she died from a massive overdose.

## By the Pool

He had jumped from his hotel balcony to escape a fire raging through the hotel. He had wrapped a towel around his face to help him breathe through the smoke and he had leapt for the pool but missed by inches.

## Putt Out

The golfer was pleased that he had won the match. He raised his putter high in the air to acknowledge the applause of the watching crowd and was struck by lightning.

## Stranded

The man was struck by a car that skidded onto a traffic island.

## Foolproof

Bob wrote a murder mystery called *Foolproof*. He was right; the murder plot was 100% foolproof. He submitted it to Sharon, his editor. Sharon was astounded; it was brilliant. She could get rid of her husband, and no one would suspect a thing. There was just one hitch; Bob would know that she had done it. She would have to dispose of Bob. Sharon killed Bob in the foolproof manner outlined in his story. She then killed her husband. Of course, then she had to dispose of the manuscript—as good as the story was, she could hardly publish the method of her crimes.

## The Tracks of My Tires

The woman was the only person in a wheelchair.

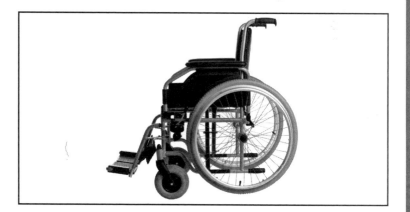

# The Deadly Stone

The man was lost in the desert. Without landmarks, he marked stones with a drop of blood from a cut on his hand. After two days of walking and out of water, he found a stone with blood on it. He knew that he was walking in circles and he shot himself rather than face a slower death.

# The Upset Woman

He was a mouse caught in a mousetrap.

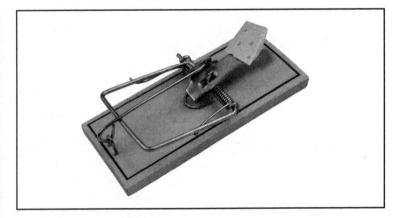

# His Own Fault

A man steals a wallet. Soon after, he is knocked down as he crosses the street. When he is brought to the hospital, he is unconscious and has lost a lot of blood. The doctors open his wallet to see who he is. They find a card stating that for religious reasons he does not want blood transfusions or organ transplants.

## Stamp Dearth Death

The man was a terrorist letter-bomber. He sent a letter bomb, but didn't put enough stamps on it. It was returned to him and it exploded, killing him.

## Murder Mystery

The man and woman lie badly injured after a car accident. The wife knows that they are both going to die and she fears that she will die first. They recently married and have no children from this marriage but each has children from a previous marriage. If she dies first, then all of the joint estate will go to his children. She kills her husband so that her children will inherit the entire estate.

## The Deadly Deal

The woman is a deep-sea diver looking through the porthole of a sunken ship. The men are sailors who were trapped and drowned. When they were sinking and realized they could not escape, they cut a pack of cards to see who would be allowed to use one bullet they had left; the other would have to suffer a slow death by drowning.

# Getting Away With Murder

The room is an elevator.

## Pack Man

It was a pack of wolves.

## Murderous Intent

She killed her sister in the hope of seeing the man again at the ensuing funeral.

## More Murderous Intent

He attached several helium balloons to the revolver and then knelt down and shot himself from above so that it looked like an execution. The gun floated away on the helium balloons. With no weapon at the scene, it looked like murder, not suicide.

# The Deadly Sculpture

He lived in a tower on a hill. Being poor, he had no money for materials, so he took the copper lightning rod from the building. He made a beautiful statue with the copper, but soon afterward the tower was struck by lightning and he was killed.

# Shot Dead

The woman was a Russian sniper who, during the siege of Stalingrad in World War II, shot several German soldiers.

# The Fatal Fish

The man's boat had capsized and he was adrift in an inflatable dinghy in a cold ocean. He caught a fish and, while cutting it up, his knife slipped and punctured the dinghy.

# The Deadly Drawing

She entered the room and saw the chalk picture outline of a body on the floor. It was the site of a recent murder and the chalk marked the position of the body.

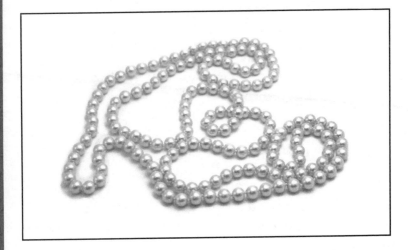

## Give Us a Hand ...

The man was a diver searching for pearls in giant clams. A previous diver had had his hand trapped in the clam, and as his oxygen ran out the poor man was forced to cut off his own hand.

## The Fatal Fall

The woman was running in the Olympics in her national relay team. She dropped the baton and her team ended up losing. When she later returned to her country, the tyrannical despot who ran it was so displeased that he had her shot.

## Death by Reading

While on a business trip, a man sends his wife a magazine. Aware of her habit of licking her finger before turning each page, he puts poison on the corners of several pages. The poison transfers from page to finger to mouth, thus killing her.

## Deadly Delivery

The man was a Christian martyr called Valentine, whose feast day was declared by the pope in the fifth century. Valentine's Day on February 14 celebrates his memory. Nowadays it is the signal for millions of valentine cards to be sent. According to estimates, one billion valentine cards are sent each year, second only to Christmas cards.

# Lifesaver

The man was a hostage taken by kidnappers. Those who paid his ransom needed proof that he was still alive. He held a copy of the day's newspaper against his chest and was photographed to prove he was alive. Thereafter, the ransom was paid and the man was released.

# The Lethal Lie

The man was captured and being interrogated by the Mafia. He had stolen a huge amount of money from them and hidden it away. However, he did not speak their language, and they did not speak his, so they had to use an interpreter. Through the interpreter, they tell him that if he speaks the truth, he will not be killed. Then they tell him (all through the interpreter) that if he does not tell them where the money is, they will kill him. In fear, he tells the interpreter that the money is hidden at a certain address. The interpreter then says to the Mafia, "He won't tell you because he doesn't think you have the guts to kill him." So they take the man out and shoot him, and of course the interpreter later collects all the money.

## Broken Match

He and a number of other passengers were making a balloon trip in a desperate attempt to escape from a country. The balloon had to lose weight to stop it from crashing. He drew the short match and had to jump.

# The Man Who Hanged Himself

He climbed on a block of ice, which then melted.

## The Music Stopped

She was a circus tightrope walker. Her most daring act was to cross a high wire while blindfolded. The band played while she crossed and when the music stopped it was the signal that she had reached the end of the wire and could safely alight. Unfortunately, one day the conductor was taken ill at the last minute and the stand-in conductor, unaware of the importance of the timing, ended the music just a little too soon. She stepped off the wire to her death.

# Suicide

The man is a lighthouse-keeper. He woke up in the darkness with a nagging feeling that he had forgotten something. He turned on the radio and heard a report that a ship had crashed onto rocks with great loss of life. He realized that it happened because he forgot to start the light that night.

# The False Confession

Bob was on death row, and due to be executed. Fred approached him with an offer. If Bob agreed to confess to a crime that Fred had committed, Fred would give Bob's family $500,000. Bob agreed.

# Available in 2011

Hall of Fame
**LATERAL THINKING**
**PUZZLES**

*Albatross Soup and Dozens of Other Classics*

Paul Sloane & Des MacHale